Chinese Tale Series

中 国 神 话 故 事

Nv Wa Mends the Sky

女 娲 补 天

Adapted by Wang Yangguang

Translated by Liu Yonghou

Illustrated by Li Chunming and others

改编　王阳光

翻译　刘永厚

绘画　李春明　王　鑫　顾景一

　　　严文胜　宋春燕　赵　勋

DOLPHIN BOOKS

海 豚 出 版 社

First Edition 2005

ISBN 7-80138-531-4

© Dolphin Books, Beijing, 2005

Published by Dolphin books
24 Baiwanzhuang Road, Beijing 100037,China

Printed in the People's Republic of China

Long long ago, the world was wrapped in total darkness and looked just like a very big egg.

在很久很久以前，世界被一片黑暗重重包裹着，就像一个巨大的鸡蛋。

A giant, named Pan Gu, cut the egg into two with a big axe.

一个名字叫盘古的巨人，用斧头把这一团混沌劈开了。

The clean light air turned into the blue sky, while the dark heavy air became the yellow ground. Fearing that the earth and the sky would mix together again, Pan Gu raised the sky with his hands.

洁净的轻气变成了蓝蓝的天空，昏暗的重气变成了黄色的土地。盘古怕天和地会合在一起，他就用双手一直托着天。

However, one day, Pan Gu became exhausted and collapsed to the ground. Since then, he could never stand up again, but the sky and the earth never mixed together once more.

终于有一天，盘古实在是太累了，"咚"的一声，倒在了地上。盘古再也没有站起来，天和地再也没有合起来。

Many years passed, Pan Gus's limbs turned into mountains, his muscles into fields, and his blood into rivers.

多年以后，盘古的四肢变成了高山，肌肉变成了田地，血液变成了河流。

His eyes became the sun and the moon, and his hair became the stars in the sky and trees and flowers on the ground...

他的眼睛变成了太阳和月亮,飘到天空中的毛发变成了闪烁的繁星,洒落地面的变成了郁郁葱葱的花草树木……

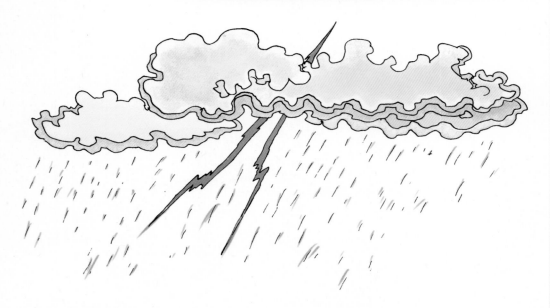

His breath turned into the breeze,and his snore into thunders while his sweat became the drizzle.

他的呼吸变成了和缓流动的风;他的鼾声变成了隆隆的雷鸣;他的汗水变成了淅淅沥沥的小雨。

The world has become a brand-new one.

世界从此焕然一新。

At the sight of the
new world, a beautiful
and kind goddess called Nv Wa
was also attracted to come down on the earth.
However, she felt the beautiful world was
deserted and lacked something.

　　善良美丽的女神——女娲，看到了世间的新气象，也被吸引来到了大地上。她看到大地景色虽美，但到处充满了寂寞和荒凉，似乎还缺少了一些什么。

" How could I change the lifeless world?" Nv Wa thought. Time passed quickly, but she still failed to find a good way.

"怎样让世界变得充满生机呢？"女娲思索着，可很长时间过去了，她还是没有想出办法。

One day, Nv Wa took a stroll along the Yellow River.

一天，女娲漫步到黄河边。

When she saw her beautiful reflection in the water, she suddenly got an idea and became very happy.

河水倒映着她美丽的身影，女娲突然有了主意，不禁高兴起来。

Nv Wa decided to use the mud to make clay dolls after her own model. A great number of clay dolls were soon made.

　女娲决定用河边的泥巴按照自己的形象来捏泥人，不一会儿就捏好了好多的泥人。

Nv Wa breathed air to those small clay dolls and they came to life immediately.

女娲朝着那些小泥人吹口气，小泥人马上就"活"了起来。

Nv Wa breathed masculine air into some dolls and made them men who were brave and strong. She breathed feminine air into others and made them women who were kind and beautiful.

女娲朝其中一些人身上吹了阳气，他们就成了男人，男人勇敢坚强；她又朝另外一些人身上吹了阴气，她们便成了女人，女人温柔善良。

These men and women sang
and danced around Nv Wa,
and the whole world was
full of life.

　　这些男男女女围着
女娲欢呼跳跃，给大地
带来了勃勃的生机。

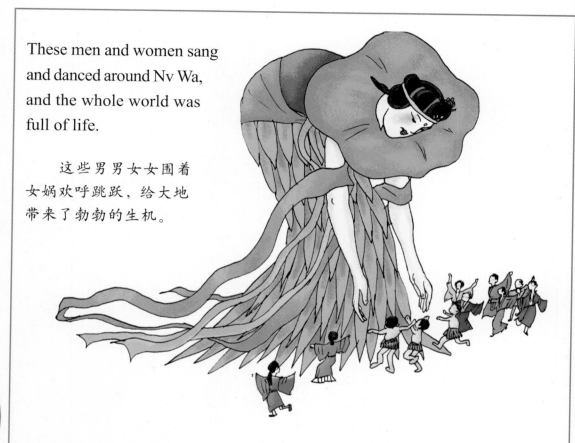

They all called Nv Wa Mother,
and some plunged into Nv
Wa's arms.

　　他们都围着女娲叫
"妈妈"，有的还钻进了
女娲妈妈的怀里。

Nv Wa molded day and night until her figures hurt. However, the clay dolls were still not enough.

　　女娲日日夜夜不停地捏泥人，手指都磨破了，可是捏出的泥人还是太少了。

Nv Wa figured out a good way to make dolls. She dipped a vine into the mire until the vine was full of mud.

于是，她想出了一个好办法。把一根藤条放进河底的淤泥里转动，藤条的上面裹满了泥。

Then she splashed mud onto the ground.
The mud splashes all became lovely
little people.

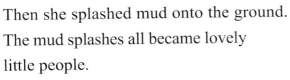

接着，女娲提起藤条
向地上一挥。藤条上
抖落下来的泥点
就变成了一
个个可爱的
小人。

Nv Wa was very happy with more children.
She continued to splash the mud, running over
mountains and plains.

看着自己
的孩子越来
越多，女娲高
兴极了！她不
停地翻山越岭，
挥舞着手中的
藤条。

Soon the world teemed with human beings.

就这样，大地上到处都是人了。

Nv Wa set up the marriage system, letting men and women get married, so they could give birth to more children, and human beings could live on.

女娲为人类建立了婚姻制度，让男人和女人结合，生儿育女，人类从此能够繁衍生息。

Nv Wa left their children and returned to heaven. From then on, people labored in the beautiful world and led a happy and peaceful life.

女娲离开了自己的儿女,重新回到了天上。人类从此在土地上辛勤劳作,过着安静美满的生活。

However, one day, a deafening sound woke up Nv Wa who was fast asleep.

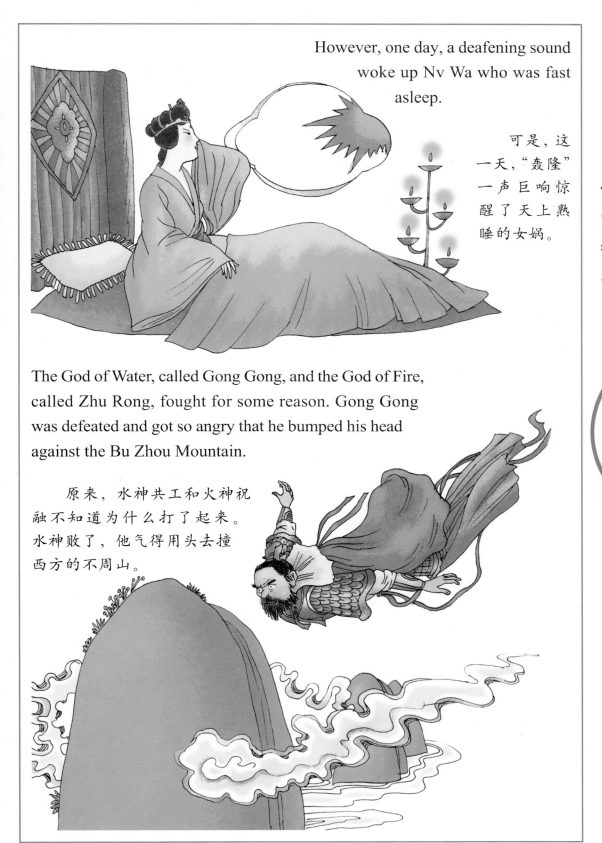

可是，这一天，"轰隆"一声巨响惊醒了天上熟睡的女娲。

The God of Water, called Gong Gong, and the God of Fire, called Zhu Rong, fought for some reason. Gong Gong was defeated and got so angry that he bumped his head against the Bu Zhou Mountain.

原来，水神共工和火神祝融不知道为什么打了起来。水神败了，他气得用头去撞西方的不周山。

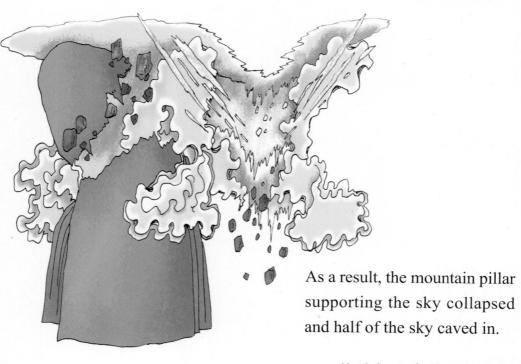

As a result, the mountain pillar supporting the sky collapsed and half of the sky caved in.

结果把这座撑天的大柱子撞塌了。

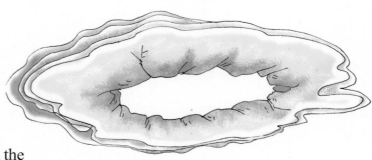

A huge hole appeared in the sky at once, and the earth was also spilt open.

顿时，天上出了一个巨大的窟窿，大地也被震裂了。

It was lightning and thundering. A heavy rain began to pour down from the hole to the earth. The whole world became an ocean and people would be drowned in no time.

天上电闪雷鸣，大雨从窟窿里倾泻而下。瞬间大地上洪水肆虐，一片汪洋，眼看人类就要被淹灭了。

In the meantime, flames were shooting up from the openings of the earth and were burning people's houses and crops.

这时，大地开裂，喷出熊熊的火焰，烧毁了人们的房屋和农作物。

Fierce dragons and wild beasts also came out to feed on mankind, and many people lost their lives.

猛龙怪兽也趁机出来残害百姓，很多人丢掉了性命。

When Nv Wa witnessed such a big disaster her children were suffering, she was bitterly grieved. She decided to save her children from the disaster. She lifted a huge stone and flew into the sky, trying to block the hole.

眼见着孩子们正在遭受苦难，女娲心痛不已，她决心拯救他们。她抱起身边的大石头，想飞上天用它堵住天上的大窟窿。

However, the rain was so heavy that she and the stone were all hurled down.

可是，雨实在是太大了，女娲连着石头都被冲了下来。

Nv Wa hurried to the Yellow River and picked up many five-colored stones from the water, and then brought them back to the sky.

女娲急忙来到波涛汹涌的黄河边。她从水中挑选了许多五色的石头，然后把它们带回到天上。

Nv Wa put all the five-colored stones into a huge pot, and then set fire under the pot. The stones melted and became dense liquid.

女娲支起了一口大鼎，燃起熊熊的烈火。女娲把五色石放进大鼎，五色石渐渐熔化成了粘稠的液体。

Nv Wa began to mend the holes of the sky with the liquid.

女娲用这些熔化了的液体一点一点把天上的窟窿补了起来。

She kept patching and filling for nine days and nine nights.

女娲不停地补呀补呀，九天九夜过去了。

The sky was at last mended and looked exactly like what it used to be. The sun rose again, and the colorful clouds appeared in the sky.

天终于补好了，和原来一模一样，一点也看不出修补过的痕迹。太阳又升起来了，天边出现了五色的云霞。

But Nv Wa was worried that the sky without pillars would fall down and the misfortune would overtake her children again.

　可是，天失去了原来的支柱，女娲担心天还会再塌下来。

Therefore, Nv Wa arrived at the East Sea.

于是，女娲来到了东海。

She caught a 10,000-year-old huge turtle and cut off its four legs.

她捉来一只万年的巨龟，斩下了它的四只脚。

Nv Wa used the turtle's four legs as the pillars to hold up the sky. The sky became steady again.

女娲把这四只脚当作擎天柱，撑起了天空。这下，天又稳稳当当了。

After that, she killed a huge dragon that had injured and killed many people, and then threw it into the crack of the earth, so the earth was filled up.

女娲一刻也不休息，她杀了残害生灵的巨龙，把龙投到大地的裂缝中，大地被填平了。

Then, the great mother went into a forest and used the ashes in the forest to block up the dashing flood.

接着，这位仁慈伟大的母亲来到山林中。她用山林中的灰烬堵住了汹涌的洪水。

Finally, the earth became peaceful and calm again.

终于，大地恢复了平静。

When Nv Wa saw mankind free from the disaster finally, she smiled delightedly.

人类终于摆脱了灾难，女娲欣慰地笑了。

The earth was full of peace, and people could live happily again.

大地充满了祥和欢乐的气息，人们又可以安居乐业了。

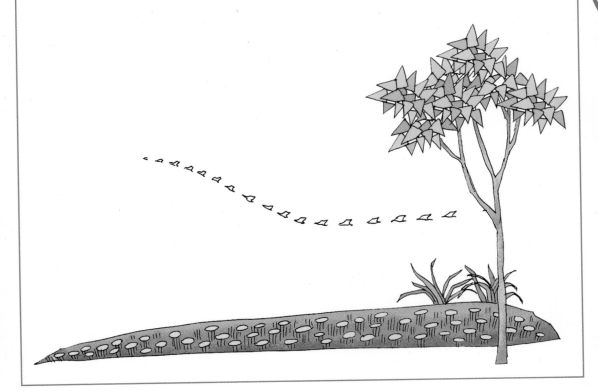

Nv Wa also invented a musical instrument by using 13 bamboo pipes and a gourd, and patiently taught people how to play it. From then on, beautiful music could be heard on earth.

为了给人类的生活带来更多的欢乐，女娲找来了竹子和葫芦。她把十三根竹管子插在葫芦里做成了笙，耐心地教人们如何吹奏，从此到处可以听到愉快的乐曲声。

When people were about to thank their
mother, Nv Wa had already gone.

当人类要感谢他们的
母亲时，他们却发现女
娲不见了。

They looked up and saw Nv Wa riding on the beautiful
clouds and flying to the heaven.

抬头一看，只见她乘着五彩云霞飞上天了。

图书在版编目 （CIP）数据

女娲补天 / 王阳光改编；李春明等绘；刘永厚译.
北京：海豚出版社，2005.10
（中国神话故事）
ISBN 7-80138-531-4

Ⅰ. 女... Ⅱ. ①王... ②李... ③刘... Ⅲ. 图画故
事—中国—当代—英汉　Ⅳ. I287.8

中国版本图书馆 CIP 数据核字（2005）第 115094 号

中国神话故事
女娲补天

改编：王阳光
绘画：李春明　王　鑫　顾景一
　　　严文胜　宋春燕　赵　勋
翻译：刘永厚
社址：北京百万庄大街 24 号　　　邮编：100037
印刷：北京雷杰印刷有限公司
开本：16 开（787 毫米 × 1092 毫米）
文种：英汉　　印张：2.5
版次：2005 年 10 月第 1 版　2005 年 10 月第 1 次印刷
标准书号：ISBN 7-80138-531-4
定价：15.00 元